Parable of the Mustard Seed

WRITTEN AND ILLUSTRATED BY

Helen Caswell

ABINGDON PRESS
NASHVILLE

READ MATTHEW 13:31-32

Library of Congress Cataloging-in-Publication Data

Caswell, Helen Rayburn,
   Parable of the mustard seed/written and illustrated by Helen Caswell.
      p.   cm.—(Growing in faith library)
   Summary: A simple retelling of the parable that compares faith to a mustard seed.
    ISBN 0-687-30025-8 (pbk.:alk. paper)
   1. Mustard seed (Parable)—Juvenile literature. [1. Mustard seed (Parable) 2. Parables. 3. Bible stories—N.T.] I. Title. II. Series: Caswell, Helen Rayburn. Growing in faith library.
BT378.M8C37   1992
226.8'09505—dc20
                                                  92-15160
                                                AC

Printed in Hong Kong

*I*n my hand I have a mustard seed.

*I*t is so tiny that you can hardly see it.

I plant my mustard seed in a pot.

I put it in a sunny place.

I give it some water, and soon it begins to grow.

*E*very day it grows a little bit more.

*W*eeks go by . . . and it is a BIG plant.

*I*n the meadow are many more plants, all from tiny seeds.

*F*aith in God is like a mustard seed.

You can't see it, but it is very important.

*L*ike the tiny seeds, faith is full of life and beauty.